# YouTube Influencer

How To Become a Youtube Influencer, Why Influencer Marketing Matters, and How To Monetize Your Channel- For Beginners

By Jeff Abston

Copyright ©2018 by (Jeff Abston)

All rights reserved. No part of this book may be reproduced or transmitted in any form or by any means without written permission from the author.

ISBN-13: 978-1986341035

ISBN-10: 1986341038

# Table of Contents

INTRODUCTION ................................................................... 1

INFLUENCER MARKETING .................................................. 3

YOUTUBE INFLUENCER ...................................................... 7

TIPS TO FINDING YOUR YOUTUBE INFLUENCER ....... 10

HOW TO GAIN YOUTUBE FOLLOWERS ........................ 19

HOW TO GET MORE VIEWS ON YOUTUBE ..................... 21

YOUTUBE MARKETING ...................................................... 29

TIPS TO USE YOUTUBE FOR BUSINESS .......................... 35

MAKING VIDEOS AND MONEY WITH YOUTUBE ......... 38

UNDERSTANDING YOUTUBE ANALYTICS ..................... 43

CONCLUSION ...................................................................... 48

# INTRODUCTION

The ability to influence others is a highly advantageous characteristic. Influencers share a common set of attitudes which ensure consistent success. Building a strong relationship with your peers is essential in influencing their decisions. Because of this, we can say there is a certain power that comes with having influence, but what is power if there is an absence of trust? How do we earn their trust in order for us to activate our ability to influence them?

Influencers brand themselves. Influencers are not just marketers, let's face this fact; these top influencers are among the great entrepreneurs: they don't just create blogs because they have their own websites. They don't just do marketing because they could start their own businesses. Above all, they brand their own names. If you follow a certain company or a brand, it's like you are also following the face of that brand and/or organization.

One of the most popular methods when using YouTube is to partner with YouTube Influencers; top video bloggers or emerging celebrities post videos on YouTube and have a huge audience. These are the rockstars online using the social media industry. They are what we call Internet sensations. YouTube celebrities are particularly common in the beauty and fashion industries, but there are others that suit your brand and products.

If you are an upcoming brand and want to broadcast your business online, you will want to build relationships with YouTube Influencers, as they help you build a large community of customers and boosts sales. If you have product samples, it is recommended to give them to those YouTube Influencers in the hopes they will mention you in a review. A single video could have a a large impact on your sales.

# INFLUENCER MARKETING

We know that in the celebrity industry, everything is a buzz; every move a celebrity makes is huge gossip. Well, in business and marketing there's also what we call a "hot issue". There are lots of effective methods of spreading news online and "Influencer Marketing" is the one that stands out among them.

Today, we are living in a world full of marketing and e-business. When you think of doing an advertisemen, what comes to your mind? Magazine headlines? TV Commercials? I'll tell you the truth, they may not be as effective as before. Time changes and effective advertising changes too. Influencers simply speak some magic sentences on their 1-3 minute videos and Voila! Sales come true! These influencers with their extensive, large number of followers can make you stand out from those chaotic, old-fashioned advertising methods out there. On the other hand, they will also ultimately bring massive value to your brand.

**So what is Influencer Marketing?**

Before we dig deep into understanding its insights, we must first define two words:

- Influence is the ability to have an effect on behavior, development, character, and the decisions of someone on something, and even the effect itself.

- Marketing is an activity of a business to promote or sell products and services.

When the two words combine, Influencer Marketing is a type of marketing that utilize "influencers" who have the capacity to influence others to buy what are they promoting or selling.

There are two forms of influencer marketing:

Social Media Marketing: Refers to a series of actions to gain traffic and attention through social media sites.

Content Marketing: Refers to a type of marketing that involves creating, publishing and sharing online material such as videos, blogs and social media posts. It doesn't always promote a brand but simply generates interest in its products and services.

Both have different definitions, but they seem to be connected.

Influencer marketing might be a hot issue right now, but it is not new at all; in fact, influencer marketing has been alive since we first discovered social media sites. Celebrities, sports enthusiasts, and leaders were our first influencers in their particular fields, and brands would partner with them to promote their products and services. Here are the good characteristics Influencer Marketing is armed with:

**Influencer Marketing is Unique**

Social media communication has already given everyone the opportunity to voice their own perceptions. Anyone with the ability to speak, who has an Internet connection is welcome to share their content. Anyone who owns a smartphone can produce high-quality photography and share it with the world thorugh their personal social media accounts. Whoever among them has the greatest and most intriguing engagement will rise and might become an influencer.

**Influencer Marketing is Authentic**

Yes, you read it right. Have you seen an advertisement online regarding the easiest way to lose that sloppy fat in your belly? Have you ever felt a single cell in your body believe those advertisements? Or, have you seen an advertisement on TV regarding a soap that could immediately whiten your skin after just one wash? How possible is that? No offense, but this is what makes Influencer Marketing authentic and more effective than the traditional advertising you see online, in TV commercials, etc.

Influencer campaigns are more organic and genuine than those traditional advertisements you encounter, why? First, Influencers are visible and have experienced or used the product or service offered. They are scrutinized role models and leaders. Investing your time, effort and money on fertilizing their audience and connecting with their following is worthy as these influencers have become the most trusted sources for consumers. Meaning, people listen and believe in them.

**Influencers help with your Brand image**

Social media has the ability to drive traffic to your website. It can create a much stronger bond between you and your customers, boost your SEO and could generate media coverage. Influencers are absolutely your "Superman" when you need a hand to promote your brand's name and create a big buzz on various social media sites. They will help you target the right demographic, grow your social media network, share ideas regarding creating content and boost your SEO.

**Influencer Marketing is Cost Effective**

If you are tired already of posting some flyers anywhere in your area not getting any sales at the end of the day, Influencer Marketing is the best method for you. Although there is no fixed price when it comes to Influencer Marketing, either you offer them a free item, pay them by performance, or go for "flat rate" pricing. But I tell you, influencer marketing has the best ROI. A lot of research has already proved that it is bound to be more affordable and effective than traditional advertising.

Influencer Marketing is not about celebrity endorsements and paid gambling. It is about the authenticity of the influencer, uniqueness and the genuine relationship between the influencer, the brand and the audience/customers. That is exactly the reason why influencer marketing is different from other marketing strategies.

# YOUTUBE INFLUENCER

What is a YouTube Influencer? Well, we all know that YouTube is a huge social media platform when it comes to videography. We all get our music and audios there; we upload and share. But do we know what is a YouTube Influencer? This might sound interesting!

The word "Influencer" itself seems like a very powerful word. So when the two words are combined, it's like having a video of yourself, talking, advertising, experiencing a certain topic that could influence other people watching you.

A YouTube Influencer gets paid huge sums for speaking collaborations, engagements and even advertising your brand or product, by exposing your service or product on their videos, or they could lead traffic to your website or other social media accounts just by doing shoutouts on their videos and other social media pages.

The social space is getting louder and bigger online, and attention is becoming more greedy. Everyone might want to be an influencer but be careful, as a real influencer needs to be more patient, persistence and more positive! Especially a YouTube Influencer.

Reading a book or watching a video of some YouTube influencers and personalities can really inspire you to become an "Influencer". If you want to become a YouTube

Influencer, these tips might help you in building your name in the social media industry.

Experiment. It's really important to be unique on your own. Exploring other videos from other YouTube influencers might help a lot. Have you found their videos inspiring? Is it your passion? Make sure to choose your own niche as long as you love what you are doing and can purely present your art to the world.

**Love the Flow.** This might be the only way to keep working and improving your production. If you don't love what you are doing, then why continue? Your video would not look alive and happy if you don't love your creation.

**Interact with the Community.** When people love your video, they will surely react through comments, thumbs ups and even messaging. It's important to interact with your followers and viewers, so they will know that they are being appreciated. You are a YouTube Influencer so you should be social.

**Quality and Creativity.** Brainstorm, think of more creative ideas on how to improve your uploads. If you focus on one variant, people will think the video is boring and repetitive. Make sure to get yourself ready every day to make more videos and share your ideas and creativity, as your followers expect new offerings from you every day or every week.

**Be Patient, Be Responsible.** As your followers increase, you should be patient and more responsible to face challenges each day; you won't find a YouTube influencer who stops working for a month and goes back on track. If this happens, you might lose your followers. Update your followers, be responsible and patient in thinking other ways or ideas to show them that you are still there.

The rise of a YouTube Influencer has created scalable and lucrative communication for brands and other niches, but only if your public approached in the right manner. Knowing the glitches of being a YouTube influencer might help you learn the strategies to avoid.

# TIPS TO FINDING YOUR YOUTUBE INFLUENCER

Influencer Marketing is the process of identifying, engaging and supporting the folks who create the promotion with the most impact on your brand, products, and services. Influencers are likely to be customers because they also testify on you are promoting, or we could also call them recommenders of your products and services, because they introduce and recommend your product to the crowd. Thus, choosing the right influencer is essential.

The growth of Social media has had a huge impact on the growth of influencer marketing. I can say that YouTube is one of those huge social media platforms where we can get effective an influencer for your brand. YouTube Influencers each have their different promoted products from different brands, according to their niche. This social media site has 100 hours of video uploaded per minute and six billion hours of views per month. It is a huge place that could be right for your business. This means that YouTube is to be considered when it comes to marketing your product.

YouTube Influencers compared to mainstream celebrities are more popular among teens, largely in the U.S.. Companies are now recognizing the pros of investing in YouTube Influencers and their marketing power. There are ways you can find, identify and connect with YouTube Influencers to associate with for your brand campaign:

**Multi-Channel Networks.** A lot of talent management agencies recruit YouTube Influencers to help set up a brand campaign. Some of these companies reach out to the network of YouTube channels, find available talent, target the best influencers who fit your brand, and make deals.

Sometimes, channel owners won't get back to you directly, especially on those larger channels, so you may think that agencies are the way to connect with desirable talent; but, there is a disadvantage here, as often agencies do not fully understand the nature and specific needs of your brand. They end up offering of partnerships with popular channels not suitable for your brand, so it is not your bet.

**Influencer Platforms.** Using platforms that act as a Virtual Marketplace for connecting brands and influencers is an excellent solution. Just like the outsourcing platform UpWork, they are very similar to each other. The difference is that UpWork gives people an opportunity to submit and get proposals from freelancers, and these influencer platforms allow brands to drop their expectations and receive proposals directly from influencers.

**Reach The Talents Directly.** Brands can connect to Influencers directly on YouTube. Most of these YouTube Influencers publish their business emails on their channel's "about" page. There is also a "send a message" box available. If you do not hear back from the channel owner, you could follow up through other sources such as Facebook, Twitter and Instagram. YouTube talents are receiving hundreds or even thousands of emails daily, so your email may not easily get noticed or might be placed in the spam folder.

**Measure the Results.** If you have found the right YouTube Influencer, plan the performance evaluation, and put tracking in place. Track the campaign CPA and CPC by measuring clicks and conversions, and you need to create tracking links. Ask the influencer to use your tracking link within the video description and video annotations. You will want the link to look clean so it is recommended to use URL Shorteners.

YouTube might not be the same as Facebook, Twitter or Instagram, but it is an excellent resource or tool for Influencer Marketers. Working with a YouTube Influencer lets you harness the power and effectiveness of promotion for your brand.

## WHY DOES A BRAND NEED INFLUENCERS?

Influencers are the people who are active on social media and blogs. They are also brand advocates and topic promoters. But why are they essential to your brand? Why does your brand need influencers? Here's why:

Buyers or consumers trust recommendations from a third party, more often than from the brand itself. Admit it, you can't trust a person at a party who comes up surprisingly to you and brags about himself and spouts facts about his personality just to convince you to be a friend. S

Social media is broad showing explosive growth over past years, creating a shift in the way companies and brands approach marketing. The traditional tactics of pushing out branded content to your audience is no longer as effective as it once was. Consumers have the most power because of social media and they expect to engage with brands in "real time". Today, traditional marketing strategies take the back seat to new methods, and these new methods keep consumers engaged and attracted while driving them to take action. It is a genius idea.

The idea and strategies of influencer marketing have become hot stuff for most marketers; they open up new avenues through which you can connect with consumers directly.

The power of social influence keeps growing and social media users with influence can be more important for your brand than any other type of paid advertisement. Although it takes time and effort to execute, it is worth it.

Influencer marketing increases credibility. While establishing your authority by collaborating with influential users, you can expand your brand reach. You create the content you want, rank higher on search engine results pages and become active on social media. Influential users trust their peers or networks more than any other brand, which is why influencer mentions can are a fast track to credibility. In other words, you have just validated your positioning through the commanding presence of the promoter.

Influencer marketing helps broaden your audience. Take time to identify the appropriate influencers fit your brand or those who have the same interests and will appeal to a larger audience. Collaborating with them gives you access to a bunch of audiences that havwe the extensive potential to become consumers of your products.

Get help with your SEO. When content is created, influencers will surely link back to your site by creating a backlink. This method is a famous ensures that the number of referring domains and backlinks to your site have a strong influence on your search engine results pages or SERP rankings.

Driving leads boost sales. The higher your reach, the greater the benefit of influencer marketing. Besides, sales and leads keeps the brand's journey continuing. Having your influencer promote a discount code to their audience is a great way to encourage people to purchase your product. Surely, at the end of the day, sales will exceed more than what you expect.

In any marketing strategy, it is very much important to identify key performance indicators and measure them after your strategy becomes activated.

# WORKING WITH A YOUTUBE INFLUENCER

No platform delivers a better return on investment (ROI) than YouTube when it comes to influencer marketing on social media. Stars of these online videos are beginning to shine more than the mainstream celebrities. With their one-billion viewers, these YouTube stars are walking on the path to success, and interestingly enough, most of the audiences are teenagers.

Brands want to sell products, and connecting to a YouTube Influencer's loyal following is an effective and increasingly common marketing strategy that is proven and tested by most brands.

One of the biggest challenges a brand or company faces is how to get visibility. Should you pay for an advertisement? Influencers can make an impact compared to what an advertisement can do because the fans who engage with a specific promoter or influencer are willing to interact because of that individual.

When brands look for the best possible effective way to reach their intended audience, they have choices. A targeted ad that integrate an influencer aimed at the influencer's demographics works well; or maybe include the influencer in brand integration such that the influencer pushes traffic without advertising. It is just all about visibility and leverage.

Here are some facts about working with a YouTube Influencer:

**Get Started with Influencers**

To find influencers, there are a lot of platforms to look at. You will find listings, cost estimates for working with influencers and a tool for contacting potential candidates. This is how these platforms work and are created.

**How does the Partnership begin?**

We can't deny the fact that most of brands approach the influencer. There are lots of platforms that will connect brands with influencers and vice versa. Often, some people have more success getting brand deals than others; it has to do with the ability to be seen on the Internet.

For an example, say a brand is looking for a beauty blogger, which is your niche, but you don't come up on Google search results in other words, you are not searchable. In this case, you are going to have a hard time getting sponsorships. You need to be on some sort of list: you have to show up in search results.

**What does an influencer need from a brand to do their job well?**

Aside from the huge bucks received by an influencer, creative control is also a part influencer needs. Brands want to trust that the influencer is able to deliver with their audience. Brands can offer guidelines, but they should let the influencer develop ideas for the video. Influencers spend numerous hours outlining their own personal brand learning what their audience likes. When the brand gives the influencer all the requisite information and let the influencer take it from there, the result is, a good influencer will be able to come up with an innovative way to promote the product. Then the magic starts.

**Is the influencer the right fit for the product that is being marketed?**

Get to know what the influencer's channel is about and who the audience is by doing good research. Watch the influencer's videos and read the comments. If they have a really active channel and the influencer is doing a lot of videos elevant to your product, then it's probably the right person for you.

The special ingredient in a great YouTube Influencer campaign: just like the previous topic, it's about finding the right fit. For example, a very popular YouTube influencer in the field of beauty tutorials has 5 million subscribers and people watching every single move they make. If they were to promote a new contour palette, their follows will definitely buy that product. The more the influencer is established, the more they can stray from what they normally promote.

If a brand integrates an influencer into their campaign, the business will have a higher probability of success. For a campaign to reach the heights, you just need to let the influencer create what they want. Give them some guidelines and parameters and they will know what to do. The influencer is not taking over the whole campaign, but they will need all possible information about it so and both of you can work together.

# HOW TO GAIN SUBSCRIBERS

YouTube has the most users of all the social media networks. The large community makes it a key marketing tool for businesses to promote their websites and find potential new customers. I will now go over the main techniques to grow and develop your following on YouTube.

Some key elements in building a YouTube following:

Short punchy videos

Regular new videos

User interaction

Promote in social media

Uploading new videos regularly

Content is key when trying to build a YouTube following. If you look at many of the famous YouTubers, they all upload at least once a week, normally on a certain day. The advantage of uploading once a week shows you are dedicated to your subscribers, and in turn people will feel more obliged to subscribe to you because of the effort you put into your videos. It also means your subscribers know when your videos will come and when to check for new ones.

## User Interaction

At the end of the day, people are more likely to subscribe to you if they are involved in your videos. The best way to incorporate some form of User Interaction is by asking your viewers a question in the video, which they can answer in the comments section. This makes the viewer communicate with you, thus building a relationship between you and your viewers and subscribers.

## Ask Questions

By asking a question that can be answered in the comments, the video gets more comments, which in turn means it will go on the "Most Discussed" charts and end up with more views and hopefully new subscribers.

## Integrate with other social media

Uploading a video gives you an opportunity to talk about it on other social media platforms. You should always Tweet about the video or promote it on your Facebook or website. A written version of the video could be uploaded to blogs or expert article websites.

# HOW TO GET MORE VIEWS ON YOUTUBE

If your band's YouTube videos aren't performing as well as you would like, there are a few simple methods of improving your viewer count. This boost to your video viewers will create a larger fan base for your sound, which will lead to increased popularity for your band. Some of these methods will lead to an immediate increase in your viewers while others lead to long-term benefits.

**Method 1:**

YouTube is a form of social media. As such, collaboration between your videos and other social media outlets is important. One of the best social media networks for increasing your fanbase is Facebook. This social media outlet gives you the opportunity to embed your videos in your profile and messages to your entire social network.

By building a large social network, adding friends, joining causes or groups and playing the various networked games, you can quickly spread the message about your recent videos to hundreds or thousands of eager viewers with a single message post.

**Method 2:**

Myspace is similar to Facebook in that it is a social media network with access to thousands of possible fans. Offering ease of access for posting in the form of status messages or bulletins, and making use of Myspace as a method of promoting your YouTube videos, can easily boost your video viewer count within a few hours.

**Method 3:**

Twitter is the future of advertising. Offering quick access to thousands of followers, tweeting the links to your band's videos will spread the word about your latest releases in seconds. Twitter has become the global marketplace and people go there for entertainment and current news events. By establishing a large following in the Twitter-scape, you can increase your band's popularity and your viewing audience dramatically.

**Method 4:**

So far, the discussion has primarily been about short-term methods for a quick boost of your YouTube viewer stats. Method 4 is a long-range plan that will create results a bit more slowly but with more likelihood of sustained results. Creating a website with embedded YouTube video or links to your YouTube videos will result in increased viewer traffic over the long term as the search engines find and index your recordings. You can speed the process a little by making sure to add quality content and optimizing the site for search engine robots. By following good SEO practices, your band's website can quickly find its way into the the search engine results pages and your YouTube viewer stats should see a slow but steady increase.

YouTube video sharing is an excellent prospect for increasing your band's popularity and overall fanbase building. By using the above-mentioned methods, your YouTube videos can see a dramatic increase in the amount of viewer traffic.

## THE BEST WAYS TO INCREASE YOUTUBE VIEWS ND RETAIN YOUR AUDIENCE

Everyone uploading videos wants to increase their YouTube views. More views, more audience, more visibility, more opportunities to monetize. While views are still important, YouTube is starting to give much more importance to audience retention. This means that minutes watched is important, and in the near future, maybe even more han views. Regardless of what's most important, views or retention, the bottom line is that we want people to watch our stuff for the longest amount of time possible. We increase YouTube views by producing great video content and link building and optimization. Each one of these methods requires strategy, planning and goal setting. Right now I see 8 ways to increase YouTube views.

- Engage off the bat

- YouTube Analytics Engagement reports

- AdWords Keyword tool

- Twitter stalk influencers

- Link building from the bottom up

- Producing videos for your awesome posts

- On page video SEO

- Content circles

- Engage off the bat

The first 15 seconds of a video is crucial. This time frame is when the majority of the audience abandons watching. So you have to pay particular attention to those first seconds in your pre- production planning to increase YouTube views and decrease abandonment. Whether you produce video blogs, sketches, tutorials, whatever it is, make those first seconds "pop".

How to engage? That's a whole blog post in itself but here's are a couple of ideas. Catchy music is energetic and vibrant, much like television newscasts. Stating what the viewer will learn, experience, feel, etc. by the end of the video is very similar to the heading of a blog post; if it doesn't describe a benefit, it's not likely to retain interest.

## YouTube Analytics Engagement Reports

YouTube Analytics is chock full of great information about a channel. The problem is that if you're fresh on YouTube, there won't be much data to interpret. For now, let's assume you have some data. The Engagement Reports section of YouTube Analytics offers you a peek into the psyche of your audience. Every section--subscribers, likes and dislikes, favorites, comments and sharing--gives you a top 10 list. To increase YouTube views with engagement reports, all you have to do is produce more of what's listed on these top 10 lists. They tell you what your audience likes. For example, favoriting and sharing a video requires much more effort by the user, a couple more clicks than a like; and in my opinion, it's a much more valuable indicator of your audiences' tastes and preferences. So produce more of those top 10's, give viewers more of what they like and increase YouTube views.

**AdWords Keyword Tool**

Another crucial factor to increase YouTube views is content that is valuable to the audience. The value of a video can be determined by seeing if it answers questions, solves problems and/or satisfies a need of the viewer, NOT you the producer. To help us produce more relevant and valuable content for our audience, we can use the Google AdWords Keyword Tool to do some research into what our audience is searching for. Then with that information, we can produce videos that answer questions, solve problems and/or satisfy the needs of viewers.

**Twitter stalk influencers**

Careful, this does not mean Twitter Spam; it literally means stalking (being present while staying out of sight). So what's an influencer? It's simple, someone who can easily influence a group of people generally into taking some sort of action because of the credibility this person has gained. By Twitter stalking these people's timelines, you can get a feel for what they like, don't like; and, most importantly, you can get insight into their questions, problems and needs that you can answer, solve or satisfy. You want to discover what they need and haven't found an answer to, then swoop in, produce a relevant video (obviously related to your brand/company/mission) and tweet it in the hopes that it scratches an itch, gets you retweeted to their audiences, and in turn helps you increase YouTube views.

**Link build from the bottom up**

I've seen great success in my work to increase YouTube views by asking for collaborations with other YouTuber sand links from relevant sites. Not rocket science I know, we normally go after the people and channels with the most massive audiences, but not a good idea. Reaching out to these people is like finding a needle in a hay silo. Their inboxes are always full, time is scarce and you're petitions never get onto their radar. Who you should contact are people with just a little bit more influence, if not the same, as yours. These people and channels are mucho more accessible because they have a similar mission as you do: increase YouTube views. So they tend to answer emails, messages, comments, tweets, fan mail and even their cell phones. It is all about incremental growth from the bottom up through accessible channels.

**Produce video from your posts**

Another way to increase YouTube views is to produce video that's complementary to your own blog posts. This diverts traffic from your blog to your YouTube channel. Video complementary to your posts can add a dynamic a audiovisual component that can engage those who aren't big readers. Maybe you could make quick two-minute video summaries for those on the go, or you can go all out and describe through video complex ideas not easily understood in text.

**On page video SEO**

The titles, descriptions and tags you enter while uploading your video should be treated in the exact same way that you would those on your website. To increase YouTube views, people have to be able to find your content and titles that says SAN003498.mov or Video Blog 027.mov get you nowhere. Do some keyword research for each video topic. Once you decide on a phrase, us it early in your title. This is no different than the title tags on your site. The description could be viewed as the meta description, a great place to add longer tail phrases and keywords. If you have the ability to transcribe your videos, the description is a great place to put text. The tags are another area where you can place some researched keywords and phrases.

**Content circles**

One of the simplest and least used ways to increase YouTube views is to never let your audience abandon your channel. This is achieved through planned out content production and an annotation strategy. The idea is to place annotations within one video that, at some point, offer the ease and visual cue of "click here to watch the previous", "click here to watch the next", "click here to watch the making of", "click here to watch the... ", you get the point.

# YOUTUBE MARKETING

If you're a business looking to promote online using videos, you probably have your eye on YouTube. It is a free, fast, and easy way to get your business videos out to a massive audience. But how can you do it effectively, without overstepping the community's boundaries?

YouTube, like many websites, has a number of rules and restrictions. It is not only important to know these rules, but to follow them, as there are a number of consequences for not doing so. Accounts can be terminated at their discretion, so it's important to keep their Terms of Service in mind when approaching them as an avenue for marketing.

A few rules you'll want to live by as a YouTube user:

**1. Use your comments the right way.**

Whenever you leave comments for a YouTube video, you should use your best judgment and remember it reflects your image and business. Negative feedback or blatant spam can easily make other users avoid you. If you spam or leave foul language on a video, other users have the ability to report you.

**2. Don't spam, period.**

There are a ton of ways to abuse the YouTube system. Don't do it. While it's OK to promote yourself and your YouTube Channel, it's also against the rules to post large amounts of untargeted, unwanted or repetitive content, including comments and private messages. Steer clear of spamming with videos and links. If you want to attract a user's attention, post a video as a response instead. Spam and foul language will likely not only get your message revoked, but it may also get your account suspended.

**3. Use your own content.**

Don't be offensive or "borrow" content from a user without permission. While many users do this on a regular basis for their videos, it's not going to fly for a business. Somebody will probably come after you - and then the liability transfers from the website to your company. Don't use copyrighted music unless you hold a license to do so. (If you're having trouble finding music, do a search for Creative Commons music on Google. Make sure the music is attributed properly.) Before using music, television or movie clips, get permission to do so. If you fail to get permission, you are, essentially, stealing someone's work.

**4. Don't be misleading.**

It's unprofessional and against the rules to use misleading descriptions, tags, titles or thumbnails to increase views. While it's OK to promote yourself and your YouTube Channel, it's also against the rules to post large amounts of untargeted, unwanted or repetitive content, including comments and private messages.

> The above-mentioned rules are just a few of the many you are expected to follow when using YouTube. It is a fun community with room for everyone - business owners, MLM'ers, affiliates, and, of course, individual users. It's

best to stick with your gut if you feel that your videos or behavior may be against their policies. Protect your business and your reputation by following and respecting the rules of conduct. And enjoy being part of the YouTube community!

## KEYS TO AN EFFECTIVE YOUTUBE MARKETING STRATEGY

There are quite a few video sharing platforms available to us these days. And yet, YouTube still remains the number one site since it has the largest community. YouTube also has several free and easy-to-use tools you can access right on your YouTube channel. This makes it easy for you to promote your business and increase your visibility online.

Here is a quick overview of 5 tools that should play a key part in your YouTube marketing strategy:

**1: Video Analytics**

YouTube allows you to look at video analytics for your videos on their site and even to download more advanced reports that can be imported into Excel. You can view data for certain date ranges, world views from YouTube Insight, world referrers, and video demographics. It's easy to figure out your viewers' ages, gender, location and to determine how popular each of your videos are with this information. And guess what? It's free!

2: **Tagging**

Tags - I like to think of them as keywords - are a vital part of optimizing your video for the search engines. Pay close attention to the tags you use for each video and make sure your tags are relevant to your content.

A great way to come up with effective tags is to start a search within YouTube for your topic and see what terms pop up in the drop down box. Those that are popping up are the ones you know are already being searched within YouTube, so they are great to use as tags as well.

Take it a step further and select a few videos high in the rankings for the tags you want to use and see what additional tags they are using. If these keywords are appropriate for your topic, use them!

Using keywords in your title is also VERY important for SEO purposes. Use those keywords in your title that you KNOW you audience is looking for.

3: **The Share Button**

It may sound too simple, however, but ALWAYS tell your viewers to click the share button. YouTube allows viewers to share videos via embedding, tweeting, sharing on Facebook, or simply e-mailing the video link. Gmail users can even play YouTube videos right inside their e-mail. The Google Plus link allows you to watch videos with friends by using the hangout feature.

Even though all these feature are right there next to your video, you STILL have to encourage viewers to do the sharing. They are distracted and likely won't think of doing it themselves.

## 4: Upload a Transcript of your Video to YouTube

This is where you are going to be so happy you wrote a script! As you know, the audio portion of your video cannot currently be indexed by Google or YouTube for SEO purposes. The technology simply doesn't exist right now. I do however understand that that technology is being developed as we speak.

## 5: YouTube's Promoted Videos

Google, one of the top online advertising platforms, has integrated its marketing platform with YouTube. Well, they own YouTube. YouTube's Promoted Videos feature helps you attract customers, viewers and subscribers to your business, organization, or video channel by displaying your video ad against relevant search results and related video content on YouTube.

This is a great way to catch the eye of potential customers who might be interested in your service or product. You'll be most effective when you use attention-grabbing titles on your videos to attract the interest of potential customers.

YouTube alone can greatly influence the success of your social media marketing campaign; however, it also works well with Facebook and Twitter. With the many great tools offered, if you aren't using YouTube as part of your marketing, you are missing out on an incredible way to attract new customer.

# TIPS TO USE YOUTUBE FOR BUSINESS

YouTube - the name itself suggests it's you who tube. Then, why not make optimum use of it? Uploading personal Video on YouTube (YT) is the most popular source of entertainment. Besides, beyond always using as a fun thing, you can also use it for business; Yes, for your own business. Be it small or large, a business can always benefit from video marketing in a great way.

However, though it looks very easy to harness, actually creating videos and uploading them on YT is not that simple. There are terms and conditions and particular criteria to fulfill to get your videos uploaded on this site. YT can be the best form of video marketing, provided you follow the basics properly.

Ten of the greatest tips to use YouTube for business are discussed below:

1. Everyone knows we create video for uploading on YT. But, it's not sufficient for business purposes. You have to keep the fact in mind that video on YT should be brilliantly interesting to catch viewers' attention and the theme of the video should be rich and of public interest.

2. YT is the best marketing tool around, and through it you can post all types of information related to your product. This is the best way to let all your customers, both existing

and future, know about your products. Moreover, it looks more like a face-to-face demonstration, and without even interacting with customeres directly, you can influence their buying decisions.

3. Besides being the best marketing tool, YT serves as a good source of advertising. So, advice should be taken from a YT and video expert. This could help you develop a video that is strategically correct and serves your business purpose effectively.

4. Posting a video know-how clip about your product is another top promotional step. You can add a product review either by a YT or a video expert commenting on your product. Consequently, your product will earn more popularity as soon as the reviewer points out what's best about it.

5. A video know-how clip for first-time YT visitors will work magically as it lets people discover the best things about and the user friendliness of the product.

6. YT videos can prove to be an authentic asset to your product if you guide your staff well in adding proper authenticity to it.

7. You can shoot videos of your office that will make your customers feel connected to you.

8. You can post your YT video links to various social networks. This, in turn, works in two ways - video marketing and social media marketing.

9. You can also make a deal by asking other products to promote yours in their videos while you promote theirs, just like a link-exchange in case of search engine optimization or SEO. Such cross-promoting will help you earn more popularity.

10. Video marketing can be more attractive if you run a contest on YT. This will make more viewers go through your video while participating in the contest. This will give a vigorous boost to your business.

Just don't forget to put a socialized touch in your YT profile. You can do it by including your Twitter or Facebook profile link. So, enjoy YouTube videos and utilize its presence to boost your business. Irrespective of the type of your business or the product depth and width, the use of video marketing can boost the business you are doing.

# MAKING VIDEOS AND MONEY WITH YOUTUBE

YouTube is one of the most popular websites in the whole world. Billions of people enjoy visiting the site because you can view a lot of videos that are informative or entertaining. People can upload videos of any kind and and thousands of viewers can watch it. You may express yourself, give information, or provide entertainment. Making videos and uploading them on YouTube is a lot of fun. The good thing is that you can earn from this fun activity. You can make videos, upload them and make money at the same time, just as long as you do things right.

First, you should, of course, follow the rules and regulations of YouTube regarding copyrights and such stuff.

- You should do things legally on YouTube or your videos will be removed. Have fun making the videos. Provide good quality content to a point that many will be attracted to it. Also, be a consistent video maker and YouTube uploader. You really do not need to get fancy with your videos or overdo it with outstanding special effects, just as long as many viewers will be attracted to or entertained by them.

Anything is acceptable as long as you gain a lot of visitors because this is where everything will start. Once you have already a large number of visitors coming to your videos, then you can now plan your strategy to make money on

YouTube. You may want to apply for partnership with YouTube. They have this partnership program wherein if you are qualified to be a partner, you will earn revenues from the ads they place in your videos. Once you are a partner of YouTube, you will see ads in different parts of your videos. If one of your viewers clicks on one of these ads, YouTube will share their earnings with you.

- There are a lot of ways you can earn on YouTube. You can also earn without being a partner. It is all about planning, organizing and having a good strategy. If you have a store or products to sell, making videos to promote them could increase the percentage of possible buyers. If you are earning money through your blog or websites with ads, affiliates and other promotions, YouTube can help you with that.

It has already been proven - and it is very visible - that YouTube is very popular. Given that, it can help increase your visitors to have a link with one another by using a video or just a mere text link. This will help in building more traffic and increasing your Page Rank. You can also ask for donations for your videos. Some websites do this and it helps just as long as you have good content.

- Making videos is fun and with YouTube, it will be more fun when you can earn money. If you will become a star on YouTube and become a partner, of course, YouTube will compensate you for all your efforts and the benefits provided to the website. Learn to be web savvy and understand things like affiliates, contextual ads, traffic statistics, etc. because you can incorporate them on YouTube to earn money.

# HOW TO GENERATE PASSIVE INCOME WITH MINIMUM WORK FROM YOUTUBE

When you think of making money online through YouTube, you probably think of becoming a YouTuber. That carries the connotation of becoming an active content creator, filming lots of videos and probably building a large audience/following for your brand.

This great lifestyle allows you to make money doing something you love, while also enjoying a modicum of genuine fame. It's a lot of work and requires skill, but it's also almost always worth it.

But this is not the only way to make money on YouTube. Actually, YouTube can be set up as a very nice passive income model that will generate revenue even as you rest. You can practically automate this money-making system and find that it's still surprisingly profitable. Read on to learn how.

**Maximum Revenue, Minimum Investment**

YouTubers can make money in a number of ways. They make money from advertising their own and affiliate products, for example, but they also generate revenue from

PPC ads. These are adverts that pay out for each click, so every time someone clicks on an ad or watches it all the way through, they get a tiny amount of cash.

But while this amount may be tiny, if you can rack up thousands of views a day, then it starts to add up. If you have a YouTube video that ranks in the top spot for a very popular search term, potentially you stand to make hundreds of dollars a day.

And if that content is evergreen, then there is no reason why that video can't continue making money for a long time to come! Better yet, when you consider that you can probably make and edit a great video in a few hours, there is nothing to stop you from repeating the formula over and over again until you're eventually making hundreds, if not thousands, of dollars.

Yes, it really is that simple but here a couple of tips that will help you ensure to use precisely the correct strategy!

**Quality and Brevity**

When making your videos, think equality not quantity. It is not to say that you shouldn't make a lot of videos, rather that they shouldn't be overly long. Google encourages YouTube creators to keep their videos to around 3 minutes, as this will increase the number of complete views and thereby drive up revenues.

What's more, making your videos shorter means that you can make more videos in a shorter time frame and then have more content to upload ready to get multiple views. In this way, you can take a few days out of your regular gig, film some short videos and then upload them all to generate big revenue.

It sounds easy and it really is as long as you are making those videos high quality (you need the right equipment and good editing) and in a popular niche!

# UNDERSTANDING YOUTUBE ANALYTICS

YouTube Analytics comes in when you have started using YouTube to upload and share videos and start to wonder who is watching your videos and how can you get more views and better engagement.

When you build a dashing YouTube channel, the requirement is that you must understand who your audience is and how they engage with your videos. As luck would have it, YouTube Analytics comes to the rescue to tell you a lot more about your audience, what they like, and what kind of content you should create to become successful with them.

Here are some overviews of YouTube Analytics to help you make the most of this tool, how to get started, the insights it provides, and any possible information available in your results that you can use to improve the next time.

Get started by signing in to your Google account and navigate to your YouTube channel page; then at the top of your channel page, click on views to go directly to your channel's analytics.

**YouTube Analytics Overview**

After following the above instructions, you are now looking at your channels Analytics Overview. If you are on default settings, it will give you data for the past 28 days; but on the other hand, you can change to any period of time you wish to retrieve analytics. The data retrieved from this page is beneficial if you are looking to get a general report of how your channel is working. If you want a slight capture of your channel's performance, then Overview is the right place to go.

It should to be noted that YouTube Analytics are based on Pacific Standard Time, updated once a day and might have a delay of 72 hours. If you really want to make the most of YouTube Analytics, you might need to delve into each detailed report.

**Watch time Reports**

This is where you will find the essential analytics on YouTube. It breaks down how your different videos and their quality are keeping your audience engaged. Watch Time Reports dispense insight into the overall performance of your channel and can be used to dig deeper into the performance of individual videos.

Views are the most basic measurement of your video's success as they shows how many times your video has been watched. But they do not take into account the users that click on your content and leave immediately because views are considered of equal value no matter how long the user watched your video.

Watch time offers a more precise breakdown of the status of your content, while YouTube sums up the time people have spent watching your videos. It measures the estimated time your audience has watched your video, showing how many minutes of have collectively been viewed on your channel.

Audience Retention reveals how suitably your video is maintaining its audience. You will be able to see how much your viewers are watching each video and which parts are causing them to leave your content. It can be broken down further to see absolute audience retention and relative audience retention which shows how your video compares to other YouTube videos of similar length. Thich will help you determine which length video best fits you.

Demographics provides a comprehensive look at who exactly is watching your videos to better market them. YouTube also provides insight into the demographic breakdown of your audience by gender, age, and geographic location so that you can modify your messaging respectively.

Playback locations show any sites or pages on which your video is being viewed. One of the great things about YouTube is to create fun and entertaining videos that can be shared in different ways by embedding them in their own website or blog. The Playback locations report separates views from your YouTube page, apps, or any website in which you have embedded your videos. It will give you the estimated minutes watched and average view duration, broken down by location.

Traffic sources provide data on how your audience arrives at your video. There are different types of traffic sources including YouTube search, YouTube suggested videos that can be found on YouTube by clicking on a thumbnail, the YouTube channel page and YouTube playlist. You will be able to see how searchable your video is while diagnosing which referral platform is gaining you the most traffic.

Devices show if your audience is watching your video be it on their computer, mobile phone, tablet, or game console. You could refer to them to create shorter or longer videos that would be better viewed from a particular gadget.

**Engagement Reports**

Views are only a part of building a flourishing YouTube channel. As you are kick-starting and modifying your content to share on YouTube to build an audience, you may want to pursue which type of engagement your videos are generating.

Subscribers indicate how many subscribers you have gained and, at the same time, how many subscribers you have lost. This is important because they are the users who are watching, engaging, and possibly influencing other people to watch your videos. Monitor your subscribers on a regular basis or as scheduled to help you diagnose if you're successful in doing this. Create videos that make people come back wanting for more.

Likes and Dislikes condense the number of people who have liked and disliked your videos. It is to be noted that you should not focus on reaching your goals, but rather you should work to inspire and entertain your viewers as they are essential to your success.

Comments provide you the number of comments your video has garnered. Comments can be a great way to know your audience's perceptions of the video to engage with them better by answering their questions or responding to their comments.

Sharing emphasizes the number of times your videos have been shared and where your videos have been shared.

Annotations furnish information on your video annotation performance, their click-through and close rate. It will give you valuable information on how effective are the call-to-action features of your videos.

The essential measure of success are those audiences who are attentive to your videos, your brand, and the message behind your videos. They show their support through their likes, shares, and comments on your videos.

# CONCLUSION

There's a lot of influencer tactics out there and many of them are highly effective. Either you are paying an influencer to promote your product or working to build yourself a community of ambassadors that will take on the micro-influencer movement. You know influencer marketing can help you tackle every part of the sales funnel.

When we talk about YouTube, we usually think of YouTube as purely an entertainment platform, don't we? YouTube is a place to watch trailers for new movies or the latest music video of your favorite music icon or even the latest video that has just gone viral on the Internet. But is this the real benefit we could get from YouTube? The answer is NO! YouTube is not just an entertainment platform; it is actually a powerful platform that increase your sales in business.

These are some of the qualities and great tips to help you become an effective influencer. There are lots of benefits to becoming an influencer, but always be careful, as there are rough rocks in each milestone you can step upon while working on your success as an influencer.

Businesses could use video as an extraordinary powerful brand awareness platform, but the fortune depends on consumers. For example, a company promotes their product by launching a crazy or funny video that could become viral, not just on YouTube but on other platforms too; but building brand awareness does not guarantee future sales. People may recognize your name and consider it for future purchases. On the bright side, if this strategy is done right, huge sales and profits will be coming your way.

If you're serious about using YouTube as a marketing platform, do your research. Forget about watching TV ads and, instead, spend a few hours discovering what's hot on YouTube. Harmon says he and his staff spend several hours every day doing just that. Harmon says the goal is to begin to "recognize good ideas."

YouTube is noteworthy because it works very well in any part of most industries. It offers visual branding while it attributes traffic to your site because of the help of YouTube Influencers and YouTube itself.

www.ingramcontent.com/pod-product-compliance
Lightning Source LLC
Chambersburg PA
CBHW030053230526
45471CB00003B/1078